Netted Together

An inspiring book to remind you that God wants to be in partnership with you every step, every day.

Netted Together

Brenette Wilder

Cover designed by Brenette Wilder

Editing by Jennifer Brown, 2021

Charleen Wilder, 2019

Inquiries may be addressed to:

P. O. Box 6643, Lee's Summit, MO 64064

All scriptures are from the King James Version, and New Living
Translation, unless otherwise noted.

Copyright © 2021

by Copyright holder name

ISBN: 978-1-7378112-0-6

Printed in the United States

Preface

The individualized, devotional stories within this book are prayers netted together from my own personal sighs to encourage you. Each devotional is woven together to form a prayer mesh that prevents sighers like me from slipping through life without a Godly help-net. My sighs were longings about God's timing—"Lord, how long must I wait?" Sighs about decision-making—"What shall I do?" And, yes, sighs about daily living.

The responses to my sighs are shared with God's eye shields, that restricted my wondering thoughts and gaze toward Him. It was God who shielded me from my unsteady surroundings, teaching me dependency, agreement, and especially partnership with Him.

He taught me that when my prayers are in partnership with Him, my answers can be, too. They have the potential of being in agreement with His purpose. In the context of science, there's a similar notion of being in agreement. For instance, scientists discovered that under pressure and high temperature, ice, water, and water vapor can be present at the same time — indistinguishable. It's called the triple point. Imagine that! At triple point you can actually see all three substances thriving at the same time without dimensioning.

You may think this is crazy, but it reminded me of the response two blind men received when seeking Jesus for healing. In Matthew 9:28–29 (MSG), Jesus gave a thought-provoking response to their request to be healed. He said, "'Do you really believe I can do this?' . . . He touched their eyes and said, 'Become what you believe.' It happened. They saw."

I would like to express it this way: Are you able to dismiss the blindness of your past, the struggles of your present, and entrust the outcome of your future to be in agreement with Jesus? Can you see yourself no longer as a beggar, but as a valued resident? How about walking freely without any aid? In this moment, it became a triple point experience between Jesus and the blind men.

Agreement with Jesus says, *you have confidence that what He has spoken is already done.* So as you read these daily devotionals let your will become indistinguishable from His.

Introduction

There are many reasons why people document their thoughts. I am not a psychologist, but I read that writing down your thoughts is a good method to record your feelings. As for me, I incorporate God's scriptures into the midst of my sighs and interesting stories to be profitable for Him. Each devotional is a standalone study for a fresh look at life.

Some of the devotions came from my journal notebook that started out as a non-fiction book idea. Since the book idea wasn't going anywhere, I abandoned it, and continued to journal. However, I shifted my writing direction from front-to-back to back-to-front. At first, it felt a little strange. Even so, I continued this reversal because I wanted the feeling of a new direction of thought.

Nevertheless, an unexpected God-thing happened on April 15, 2020. The backward writings finally merged together with the front-page writings. It was bound to happen sooner or later, no pun intended. But it caught me completely off guard. It was a pivotal moment for me. It felt transitional, a time to launch something new. This pivot was validated that same day when a newspaper representative asked me to continue sending articles for their "Opinion" section.

You see, months prior, I sent her an article for the religion section, and she published it. She was also familiar with me through previous published stories about a nonprofit organization that I support. But hearing from her at a time I was contemplating my future was a God response.

I had been praying about my next steps.

"How will I continue to serve you God during a 2020 COVID-19 pandemic? How can I continue my nonprofit virtually when all of my activities have been face-to-face in the past? I'm getting too old for these types of challenges. Why do it again?"

These fearful thoughts are familiar to all of us in some form or another. But we must not let them paralyze us from moving forward.

The April 15, 2020 event was not a mere coincidence. Nor do I believe my writing abilities had anything to do with this opportunity. All I know is that God has a plan for each and every one of us. It's really not based on our abilities, our education, or our location. His plan can't be stopped even if we refuse to comply. Because when God says, "Go," we either get busy doing it or lose out on being in agreement with Him.

Table of Contents

Day 1

Faith is the netting needle that weaves each thread of your life into sufficiency.

Insufficiency to Sufficiency

Devotional scripture:

Judges 6-8

Zechariah 4:6

Then he said to me, "This is the word of the LORD to Zerubbabel, saying, 'Not by might nor by power, but by My Spirit,' says the LORD of armies. [-NASB]

Romans 8:37

But in all these things we overwhelmingly conquer through Him who loved us. [-NASB]

2 Corinthians 13:11

Finally, brothers *and sisters*, rejoice, mend your ways, be comforted, be like-minded, live in peace; and the God of love and peace will be with you. [-NASB]

How often I have gained and lost my confidence under pressure. At first, I approach the situation tall and strong, but before the day is over, I find myself short and weak, even tongue-tied with fear. What drives these roller coaster emotions? For me, I can sum it up in one word: insufficiency.

Maybe that's why I connected to a 1919 adventure story, entitled, *The Fifty-First Dragon*, by Heywood Broun. It is a story about a young pupil named Gawaine, who was enrolled in knight school. Gawaine was short on courage. So much so that the leaders wanted to kick him out of the school. His cowardice was significant enough to ruin the school's reputation, but the headmaster wasn't about to let that happen.

He said, "I think I'll train him to slay dragons." Sounds crazy, right? Instead of sending the poor boy home, he wanted to push him even

Judges 6:14

And the LORD looked at him and said, "Go in this strength of yours and save Israel from the hand of Midian. Have I not sent you?"

Ephesians 6: 10-12

Finally, be strong in the Lord and in the strength of His might. Put on the full armor of God, so that you will be able to stand firm against the schemes of the devil. For our struggle is not against flesh and blood, but against the rulers, against the powers, against the world forces of this darkness, against the spiritual *forces* of wickedness in the heavenly *places.*

further into harm's way. The headmaster thought it was the school's responsibility to build character, and it would happen for Gawaine, one way or another.

The headmaster started training Gawaine slow and easy, until pretty soon Gawaine felt confident and strong. Finally, he was ready, but the headmaster knew that more was required. He gave Gawaine a magic word -- *Rumplesnitz* -- and told him that if he said this word before battling a dragon, the dragon would have no power over him. It was a lie, but it worked! Gawaine became the best dragon slayer ever.

Spoiler alert! Let me just say, Gawaine discovered the truth and his confidence quickly reverted back to the fear that he was not enough – a fear of being insufficient.

How can one word change a coward into a world-renowned dragon slayer? Or, better still, how can a person that achieved a renowned dragon slayer's reputation change back into a coward?

One idea brought to my attention by my daughter is that Gawaine might have been emboldened by the placebo effect. Even though we don't fully understand this, in medical studies, a certain percentage of people given a placebo (fake pill) get better. Why? Because they think it is real medication and believe the medication will help.

Merriam-Webster Dictionary says, "The placebo is prescribed more for the mental relief of the patient than for its actual effect on a disorder." I surmise that the same could be true of Gawaine. His image of himself was grounded in his fears that he was insufficient and his belief that a word could help him slay a dragon gave him just the confidence he needed.

Even the greatest Biblical heroes suffer from fear. Gideon was one of them. In the book of Judges, we read how he felt insufficient when he was asked to slay the Midianites. He had no opportunity to enroll in a Midianite-slaying school. However, Judges 6:14 presented him a fast-track path straight to courageous living. The verse states, "Then the Lord turned to him and said, 'I will make you strong! Go and save Israel from the Midianites! I am sending you!'"

These were not magic words. This was God telling Gideon, "I will use your insufficiency to reveal my sufficiency." God didn't ask Gideon to be any different, like the headmaster was expecting of Gawaine. Gideon didn't have to develop new skills or use a magic word. The Lord told him to go with the strength he already had.

But, wouldn't you know it, just like Gawaine, Gideon still needed a mental relief from his cowardly state of mind. He needed a placebo in the form of a sign. In Judges 6:17-22, Gideon said to an Angel sent by the Lord, "If you find me acceptable, give me a sign that it is really you speaking to me." And so He did — fire flared up from a rock and burned Gideon's meat and bread. Then the Angel disappeared.

I believe that after Gideon saw the meat being burned up, he was ready to slay his enemy. But, when we do not act promptly, time can cause the short-term mental relief we sought after to diminish. And, once diminished, you find yourself embracing your old fears yet again. This is the case when we find Gideon seeking another sign in the form of a fleece in Judges 6:36-39.

Here's the thing. When the All-Powerful God tells you to go, and more importantly, when He tells you, *I am going with you*, then go. God will equip you by ascribing His qualities of power and might all over your thin-shell body and circumstances. Without Him, your abilities will never be enough to conquer an army. A magic word may give you a short burst of courage, but it's a counterfeit response without God.

You know this already, but I will say it again. We are His children with access to every spiritual gift He has. His arsenal of gifts and power is sufficient to slay dragons, root out fears, and even defeat Midianite situations. Now, go slay your dragon.

- Make a list of the dragons in your life.

- How do you plan to slay them?

Let us Pray:
God, we are nothing without you. It is foolish thinking to believe that we can go it alone. You are our source of strength. Help us to be victorious in all things for your namesake. Instruct us through your word. Amen

A Time to Reflect

After reading this chapter. Journal your thoughts

Day 2

Prayer is the thread that links each *Netted Together* devotional. It is the best resource to resist decaying lifestyles and it strengthens our prayer net-work.

God's Plan

Devotional scripture: Matthew 9:27-30

Is there a movie you could watch an unlimited number of times? Feelings of joy, pride, excitement, and wonder triggers each time you re-watch the show? Well, that's how I feel when I watch the movie *Hidden Figures*. Emotions of pride for the African American women who performed mathematical calculations for National Aeronautics and Space Administration (NASA), fill me to the brim.

There's one scene in particular that stays with me for days. A smart and gifted woman named Katherine Johnson worked all day to complete her rocket trajectory calculations. After she hands the work to her boss, he throws it in the trash. You can see shock engulfing her face at the sight of her hard work being tossed away. But he didn't do this out of disrespect.

NASA was trying to send a man into space and the math calculations were changing frequently. Her calculations were obsolete before the day was even over. He apologies and says, "The science team had an extraordinary task at hand. They had to look beyond the numbers and possibly through them to answer questions they didn't think to ask or know existed." And then he says one of my favorite lines in the movie: "In my mind I am already there. Are you?"

He wasn't about to let the obvious facts of unresolved math stop his foresightedness of orbiting the Earth. These were significant problems, but they were not significant enough to ground his project, his focus, or ground his belief. No way! He saw past them to the future. He, Katherine, and his staff persisted until the answer was finally revealed. And in 1961, *Mercury-Redstone 3*, also known as *Freedom 7*, orbited around the Earth and returned home safely.

Even though his quote, "In my mind I am already there. Are you?" was said in the context of math and science and orbiting the Earth, it echoed like a God-question, desperate to be incorporated into a spiritual opportunity. My mind's paraphraser reworded it this way: *The answer is fixed in God's timing. It's waiting for me to learn, grow, have patience, trust God, and believe God's plan through this trial.* Katherine's boss-problem and your problem have nothing to do with having psychic ability or wishful thinking. But it has everything to do with faith in God's ability to fulfill his promises.

This type of faith isn't easy. I know. Numerous times I have failed to trust God, only to reflect back and see His sticky fingerprints all over the situation. And each time, this backward glance built my confidence for the next trial. So, ask yourselves this question: *Do you have the mental persuasion that God's answer awaits you on the other side of what you are dealing with?*

How about, if you were blind for many years, would that diminish your confidence that God could heal you if it's in His will? Let's be honest. Some of us probably would have lost hope along the way. But, in Matt 9:28-29, The faith of two blind men were tested with a somewhat similar question when they asked Jesus to heal them. And this is what Jesus said, "Do you believe that I am able to do this?" "Yes, LORD," they replied. Then he touched their eyes and said, "According to your faith let it be done to you." (NIV)

The blind men said yes to Jesus's question. They saw past their problem and believed Jesus. And they were healed. They believed past dark days (without sight) to days of light (with sight). And they were healed. They believed what

Seen With the Eyes of My Heart
By Brenette Wilder

Scripture Eph 3:17
"And I pray that Christ will be more and more at home in your hearts as you trust in him. May your roots go down deep into the soil of God's marvelous love."

It's a dream from long ago
A dream of promise
Selective with words binding
Seen with the eyes of my heart

It's a dream of things to come
A promise of love
A promise of purpose
A promise of completion
Seen with the eyes of my heart

It is no longer I who live it
But my Savior through me
Manifested for you and me

It's a dream from long ago
And the fulfillment for today
Seen with the eyes of my heart

faith expected – dependency and trust. And they became open eyed, sightseeing men of faith. One version of the Bible stated Jesus' response this way: Jesus said, "Become what you believe." And that's exactly what they did.

As you become what you believe, trust God for your future. Receive His promises in faith. One day you will hear the ever-present, always-working God say, *you are already there.*

Let us Pray:
God, regardless of what the situation looks like, help us to trust that you are working on our behalf for our good. Give us the courage to wait for the answer when times are challenging. Thank you for interceding on our behalf. Amen.

A Time to Reflect

After reading this chapter.   Journal your thoughts.

Day 3

You were born to an eternal hope. So in life choose what will resist rot, not things that are short-lived. Choose Jesus. 1 Peter 1:3

Keep in Step

Devotional scripture: John 8:25-32

A few years ago, my husband and I took ballroom dance lessons. It was so much fun! Missed steps and injured toes were par for the course. Like all beginners, we had to learn the basics. We were shown foot placement, timing, and the proper hold. But the most important thing we learned was that one person leads and the other must follow.

John 8:28
So Jesus said, "When you have lifted up the Son of Man on the cross, then you will understand that I am he. I do nothing on my own but say only what the Father taught me.
– NLT

To give my husband credit, he was all-in. I, on the other hand, found myself breaking the cardinal rule – leading when I should have been following. Don't worry, my instructor quickly nipped this in the bud. He showed my husband how to take control by giving me strong dance signals. These signals were non-verbal ways of communicating. A firm push or an intentional pull was all it took, in most cases. With a lot of practice, it became clear when it was time to follow rather than lead.

Similarly, in life we must learn how to follow. It was Peter, in Mark 8:27-38, who strongly protested when Jesus said that He had to suffer and die. This was a Jesus leadership moment that required strong followers. However, instead of agreement, Peter expressed strong disapproval. But with a firm push and an intentional pull, Jesus quickly signaled him back in step. Listen to what He said: "Anyone who intends to come with me has to let me lead. You're not in the driver's seat; I am. Don't run from suffering; embrace it. Follow me and I'll show you how. Self-help is no help at all. Self-sacrifice is the way, my way, to saving yourself, your true self. What good would it do to get everything you want and lose you, the real you? What could you ever trade your soul for?" (MSG)

In this moment, I believe that Jesus was preparing the disciples not only for His death, but for living a surrendered life for the cause of

12

Christ. The transitional step of their life without Christ was about to happen. And the leader signaled that they had to refrain from satisfying themselves and learn self-sacrifice.

If they could follow His example of self-sacrifice for others now, then being in step with the Spirit after His death would be a cakewalk. This student-pupil lesson of giving up one's own interests to help others isn't easy, not then and not now. In fact, easy-living to achieve one's own plans isn't Jesus-living. Jesus-living is following His lead.

Let us Pray:
God, it is not always easy to stay in step with your will. So often, I want to do things my own way. Help me to find opportunities within my day to pause, read your word, and listen to your voice. I want to put you first above all things. Help me to follow your examples. Amen.

A Time to Reflect

After reading this chapter.   Journal your thoughts.

Day 4

The Lord will fight for you.

Fearless Living

Devotional scripture: Exodus 14

The poem within this chapter is so true. It rings true to my personal life. My business life. And, more recently, the 2020 pandemic. Do you remember in Exodus 14 when the Israelites were trapped between Pharaoh and the Red Sea? When they saw Pharaoh approaching from a distance, they became gripped with fear. The problem was still afar, but it was visible to their naked eye. Immediately, they became enslaved to fear, and the real them couldn't be found. Their emotions surrendered in terror to the distant problem.

But what if they dared to trust God no matter what? I know that trusting is an effort when horses are about to trample you into the Red Sea. However, verse 13 gave them a way out. It was a different approach for fearless living when under attack. Moses instructed the Israelites to stand. Watch. And see the wondrous ways of God.

What a Fear
by Liliana Kohann

What a fear has overtaken
me now
A fear bigger than my heart
It is so present here
That its heartbeat I hear

Its presence takes over
Everything around,
My world, my dreams,
And I... can't be found

I disappear
In the face of fear
And I don't know why
I can't look into its eye

Maybe I sense death...
Or maybe I fear
That once fear is gone
I... would have to appear.

God wanted to give them a testimony and a memory recall for when their backs were against the wall in the future. He wanted history to forever use their story to encourage you and I to see beyond our Pharaoh events and to see God-saving events. The Israelite's victory wouldn't be accomplished through combat, but by being a witness. God knew that the Israelites couldn't defeat Pharaoh's army, but Pharaoh's army was no match for God.

Against God, our Pharaohs become like ants to be crushed. He will not only crush their efforts, but Moses told the Israelites they would see Pharaoh's army no more. Basically, after God is done with our Pharaoh problems, we will never have to deal with them again.

So, let's not lose ourselves anticipating the worst. We have security in the One who chose us. The Chosen have a different path to follow, and it is called fearless living. We are held by God. We are protected by Him. And, we have been grafted into the spiritual family through adoption. It is our Heavenly Father's duty to help us. It is our duty to respond with dependency when Pharaoh events arise.

Let us Pray:
God, thank you for your daily protection. Your words constantly remind us that there is nothing that you won't do for those who love you and call upon your name. You are our strength and shield. When everything else falls away you are always present in the midst of our pain and in our joy. You are an ever-present God in times of trouble. Amen.

A Time to Reflect

After reading this chapter.   Journal your thoughts.

Day 5

Proverbs 31:10, "Who can find a virtuous woman? - for her price is far above rubies."

Rite of Passage

Devotional scripture: Romans 16:1-2

Recently, I read a story about a woman named Phoebe born approximately AD 56. Phoebe's story, although centuries old, 2-verses long, and embedded at the end of the book of Romans, represents women today. Her story is about hard-working women, committed to their duties. A woman, loved by all she served, but restricted in job assignments, promotions, and responsibilities. Her reward, if any, although personally fulfilling, was below the wages given to men. But her story was enough to catch the attention of God.

An inconspicuous list of heroes and greetings are listed in Romans 16. But Phoebe is the first person mentioned in verses 1-2 recommendations. If you're not careful, you will miss how her simple contribution impacted the world.

Historians tell us that Phoebe, a dedicated church worker, carried a letter, now known as Romans, from Cenchrea, to the believers in Rome on behalf of Paul. At the time, she had no idea how a *yes, send me* response would impact what we read in the Bible today.

Paul's recommendation of Phoebe lets us know his affirmation of her character. He says, "I recommend to you our sister Phoebe, who is a servant of the church which is at Cenchrea, that you receive her in the Lord in a manner worthy of the saints, and that you help her in whatever matter she may have need of you; for she herself has also been a helper of many, and of myself as well." In other words, *I am entrusting Phoebe into your care. Treat her like family. Get the bedroom ready. Cook the best Roman cuisines. Make her feel right at home, because she has been authorized by the Holy Spirit to serve and bring you good news.*

Staying the course of helping others, day-in and day-out, set the stage for Phoebe's rite of passage into service. Romans describe her as a servant, kind, a Saint, and generous. Some versions of the Bible refer to her as a deaconess, others as a servant or succor ready to give aid wherever she was needed. She was unprotected by law as a woman, marginalized in a society dominated by men, and restricted to serving mostly women and children. However, in God's sovereignty, He uses Paul's inspired letter and Phoebe's obedience to move her into the Romans Hall-of-Salutation Fame.

So, what if your name is never attached to a bestseller like Romans or you never see your dreams fulfilled? Should you abandon your service? Should you stop keeping on? By all means, keep going! Stay the course. Do what Phoebe did. Have faith. Push through your weariness. Don't worry about the self-recognition. Share the word of God. Help others. Because following God will always lead to your rite of passage for Him, in this life or in the next.

Let us Pray:
God, I pray for women all over the world. She may be mothers, sisters, daughters, wives, young or old that are feeling helpless or undervalued. Open her eyes to see what you see. Help her to see that she is strong, beautiful, energetic, hard-working, trustworthy, smart, and valuable to you. She helps those that can't help themselves. She prays for the weak. She feeds the hungry. Let her know that nothing she does is overlooked by you. Remind her each day that you have a glorious purpose for her. Amen.

A Time to Reflect

After reading this chapter, what is God saying to you?

Day 6

Making personal decisions can be challenging. Go slow. Seek God. He loves you and longs to be netted together in unity with you.

A Simple Model to Follow

Devotional scripture: Psalms 32:1-9

The Lord really wants to help you manage big and small decisions. So much so, that He's given us a manager called the Holy Spirit that's in charge of advocacy, intercession, and decision support. Call on Him for direction. Ultimately, His job is to lead you in righteous living.

However, if you need another approach, look to Jesus. He used a simple decision-making model during His ministry. It's a one-step process revealed in John 5:19-20. *Jesus only did what the Father said,* plain and simple. He didn't independently take on His own agenda. The same relationship is true of the Holy Spirit. The God-Heads are unified in their efforts. They are not a secret society that conceals their purpose from mankind. Quite the opposite. From the beginning, God has been inviting mankind into His plans to reflect Himself and to help you make Godly choices.

> *Genesis 1:26, And God said, let us make man in our image, after our likeness: and let them have dominion over the fish of the sea, and over the fowl of the air, and over the cattle, and over all the earth, and over every creeping thing that creepeth upon the earth.*

> *Psalms 32:8, I will instruct you and teach you in the way which you should go; I will advise you with My eye upon you.*

The word "teach" in Psalms 32:8 paints a visual portrait of understanding our life trajectory. In this case "teach" is symbolic with someone shooting an arrow or aiming with controlled precision. I believe that the arrow represents us and the archer represents God. The skilled archer (God) releases his bow in the direction *He chooses.* And prayer is the method for you to know the way. Prayer is the key to knowing God-choices.

Become the arrow. Be strong, sturdy, and straight. Don't resist the archer's pull on your life. Surrender to the trajectory like the arrow. And, know this: God will keep his eye on you at all times. He looks

24

ahead and sees all. He never loses sight of the arrow. The approach to the target may be a hard undertaking but you will be kept by God's watchful eye as you fulfill His purpose. And by surrendering to the Archer, your choices will become a God-surrendered choice.

Let us Pray:
God, when we have to experience dark and frightful times in our lives, help us to know You will strengthen us to endure through them. Keep your watchful eyes upon us at all times. We know that you have the final word and have equipped us with your Spirit.

Ephesians 6:10- 12 … "Be strong in the Lord and in his mighty power. Put on all of God's armor so that you will be able to stand firm against all strategies of the devil. For we are not fighting against flesh-and-blood enemies, but against evil rulers and authorities of the unseen world, against mighty powers in this dark world, and against evil spirits in the heavenly places." Amen.

A Time to Reflect

After reading this chapter, what is God saying to you?

Day 7

God of Creation has not forgotten you.

A Place of Retreat

Devotional scripture: Psalms 46:1

God's love for us started at the beginning of time. His precision to detail and His foresight to our needs reflects His creativity and purpose of design. Everything He made was netted together in harmonious unity for our needs. His voice carried commands that gave birth to life. He transformed nothingness into usefulness. He separated the seas from the land. He placed an expanse between heaven and the earth. Darkness gave way to light which in turn gave way to days and weeks. Creatures were made. Man was made. And everything that God beheld was declared excellent in every way.

God, the mighty one, the powerful, and creator pulled off the miraculous to reveal His glory. It was a creation fully loaded with perks. Perks such as garden-to-table food obtained from fruit-bearing trees and seed-bearing plants. Beautiful beaches and skylines reflecting God's nature. An earth with every kind of animal. God of creation did all of this. It all belongs to Him. And he stands ready to protect all that he molded into existence.

In the book of Psalms, we can find David seeking this protection many times. He spoke honestly to God about his despair of being hunted by Saul and others. David knew that the Creator would never step aside when His God-fearing creation was in distress. That's why in Psalms 46:1, David said it didn't matter if earthquakes shook the mountains into the sea. It didn't matter if a tsunami caused the sea to roar. *Let the oceans roar and foam; let the mountains tremble*, David says. God lives among His creation in good times and during hard times. David admitted to the commander in charge of earth and Heaven that God was his refuge in all things. He found retreat in his Savior. David knew no adversity could conquer him without the creator's permission.

In like manner, my mother, who was widowed with eight children to feed and clothe, spent decades in the cottonfields of Arkansas, chopping and picking cotton. With this much pressure of survival, she and countless other women within her economic bracket could have

28

easily missed their value to God. But, like David, they also sought protection in God.

The wage system provided below low minimum wages with no opportunity to keep any of the crops or food they sharecropped. No doubt they saw others progressing while their life remained stagnant. They saw people living in extremely comfortable homes while their meager houses were patched and tattered. Yet, still in their suffering they did everything right. They never let go of their faith in God. Their place to thrive was found in God. They were able to experience peace and joy regardless of their circumstances.

The God of Creation had not forgotten them, nor had He forgotten David. Their sweet fragrance of trust and perseverance caused God, in turn, to gaze downward to what He had made. He saw their hardship. He knew their struggles. He saw their lack. And He smiled in response to their endurance and trust. I liken this smile to a creation moment when God said, "It was very good." Your circumstances may not be good right now, but your faith can be very good in God's eyes. So, as you are going through, draw the attention of God in faith, and keep your eyes open for a safe place of retreat.

Let us Pray:
God, your arms are strong, and at the same time so comforting. When you are near, I feel such peace. When you speak, you remind me that I am your daughter. I am beloved by you. I am protected. I am not forgotten. You delight in me. No matter the storm. No matter the winds. No matter the thunderous roars, I can find a safe place to hide and be cared for. Amen.

A Time to Reflect

After reading this chapter, what is God saying to you?

Day 8

Stay encouraged! Everything belongs to God and is under His watchful eyes.

Shaking Things Loose

Devotional scripture: Haggai 2

Gardening television shows are some of my favorites. The idea of growing trees or vegetables from a seed is life-giving to me. I enjoy learning about new techniques that yield delicious or beautiful plants. For example, one day while looking at a video online, I learned that shaking your fruit tree before it starts to bud produces more fruit. They say it loosens the fruit vessels that carries the sap to the buds, thus enhancing the opportunity for more fruit.

Years ago, I learned a different tree-shaking use that many of us may be more familiar with. It wasn't done to increase fruit growth or production; it was done as a harvesting technique. We shook the tree to retrieve some of the luscious and sweetest fruit positioned outside of our reach.

But there's another shaking talked about in the book of Haggai that wasn't meant to satisfy taste buds. It was meant to rebuild a temple where God will give peace. In Haggai 2:6, God shares the type of shaking He is planning. "For the Lord Almighty says, in just a little while I will begin to shake the heavens and earth—and the oceans, too, and the dry land. I will shake all nations, and the desire of all nations shall come to this temple, and I will fill this place with my glory, says the Lord Almighty."

He's letting us know that everything on earth belongs to Him. Nothing is beyond His reach when He wants to rebuild or give peace. Making your latter days better than your first days may require using His money, His land, His dreams, or His house. And unfortunately, because our handgrip can be a little tight, a little shaking may be involved to break loose some things.

I don't want to be a Debbie Downer, but the 2020 pandemic looked like a prelude to an unwanted shaking. Unwanted because of the uncertainty of the future and how it affects every part of our lives. Our home life is being shaken, our faith is being shaken, and our ability to support our families is being shaken. But, here's the thing: God wants the most important thing that belongs to Him. He wants you.

And he will use whatever means He chooses to accomplish His purpose of drawing your ripe heart back to Him.

Using an analogy from my peach-picking days; keep in mind that low hanging fruit is easily accessible, but treetop fruit or even treetop experiences require a little shaking.

So even though things seem challenging, stay encouraged. Everything that He shakes loose will be used to rebuild something new, different, and better.

Let us Pray:
God, my future is better with you. So if your shaking will bring better opportunities with you, then shake, Lord. If you want my heart, the most important thing that I can give you, then shake, Lord. I know you don't desire to hurt me and will release from your hands something that will work together for good. I invite you to create in me something new. Amen.

A Time to Reflect

After reading this chapter, what is God saying to you?

Day 9

"...Not by might, nor by power, but by my Spirit...
Zechariah 4:6."

Expect Victory

Devotional scripture: Zechariah 4

When I am given a God-assignment, I *expect* to be victorious. Not once do I attribute my victories to my strength or my ability to overcome a situation. Simply put, I am weak and inadequate. It is not my background that makes me expect victory. It was grace that brought me through my low-income upbringing and grace continues to follow me. You can be upper, upper-middle, middle, lower-middle, or lower class; none of it makes a difference when you are on assignment from God. The banner I am raising before you today says, "I expect to win because of who fights for me and who I fight for."

It was General George Patton that said, "I am a soldier, I fight where I am told, and I win where I fight." General Patton frequently gave speeches to motivate his troops. In WWI and WWII, he urged men into battle. They were ordinary men with ordinary jobs, such as cook, milkman, or laborer. They were men with various positions of status. They were also men facing wartime and gripped with fear. And a good leader knows just how to rally his troops before they have a chance to be overtaken by fear.

Just like General Patton's men, we need encouragement and strong leadership from someone who truly understands our situation. This person should know our mission and have the ability to help us master a healthy response to push through despite the difficulties. And, Zerubbabel, the Jewish Governor of Judah during the reign of Darius, and a descendant from the Davidic line, knew this very well.

After being taking into exile by King Nebuchadnezzar to Babylon for approximately 70 years, the Israelites and Zerubbabel were now returning home to Jerusalem and cities located in Judah. One of their first task upon arriving was to rebuild the Temple that was in ruins. However, the governor west of Euphrates tried everything to get them to stop building. "Who gave you permission to rebuild this Temple and finish these walls?" he demanded.

Zechariah 4:7

Therefore, no mountain, however high, can stand before Zerubbabel! For it will flatten out before him! And Zerubbabel will finish building this Temple with mighty shouts of thanksgiving for God's mercy, declaring that all was done by grace alone."

In a vision, God gave Zechariah a vision for Zerubbabel regarding his assignment to rebuild the temple. God told him no physical actions would be needed against his enemies trying to stop his work. "Not by might, nor by power, but by my Spirit, says the Lord Almighty— you will succeed because of my Spirit, though you are few and weak," Zechariah 4:6, LTB. In other words, *I got this. If you were really strong enough to handle this problem, no mountain would be too difficult for you to climb. But it's my Spirit that gives strength, vigor, and endurance. And I will speak to the mountain before you and cause it to flatten!*

If Zerubbabel couldn't flatten a mountain in his own strength, what about you? Do you think you have it all under control? Do you think your skills are enough? The answer is no! Without God, you and I can't complete anything. Zerubbabel's human strength wasn't enough and neither is ours. If we were that strong, God wouldn't be able to get the glory and we wouldn't need Him.

So, what should we do? I recommend following Zerubbabel's example. Follow God's instructions and save your strength for the celebration. Start your victory laps at the beginning of your assignment. Continue your laps through the middle and finish with a great finale. Incorporate shouts like, *God bless it!*; *Grace be to God for His mercy!*; and, *Thank you, Jesus, for my victory!*

This is how you win even if it looks like you are losing: 1) Know who's in charge. 2) Know who fights for you. 3) Know who you fight for. 4) Know how to give thanks before the battle is over. That's how to *expect victory* regardless of the circumstances. If victory is near or far, always expect to win when God is calling the shots.

Let us Pray:
God, I am thankful that you fight for us. Too often we exhaust our energy worrying or trying to solve the problem. Your word tells us that God assignments will be defended by the Spirit of God. Halleluiah! Praise the Lord! Amen.

A Time to Reflect

After reading this chapter, what is God saying to you?

Day 10

When others say, "I can't", love says, "I will and I can".

Pursue Love

Devotional scripture: Hebrews 4:15-16

The first few months of 2020 were challenging. Communities were maneuvering around a number of different obstacles. Once we got over one hurdle, another one quickly appeared. Our inability to manage multiple obstacles simultaneously interfered with our ability to win in a timely manner. Clearly, the first hurdle of COVID-19 came unexpectedly. We had no time to train or prepare. This disturbance put us in last place before the race began. But the second hurdle—the most important one, in my opinion—feels like one we've been jumping over for centuries. That hurdle is the pursuit to love one another.

During a time when racial mixing was taboo, the friendship of two men found a way to reach across racial barriers. In 1965, a white football player named Brian Piccolo, who was recruited as a free agent for the Chicago Bears, became best friends with an African American teammate named Gale Sayers. It was an unlikely friendship, during unlikely times of segregation. It was the first time in NFL history that a black and white player roomed together. All eyes were on them. Blacks and whites typically lived separately, ate separately, and socialized separately. Relationships were superficial, approached cautiously, or sometimes obtained in secret. Amazingly, at the height of the civil rights movement these men pulled off the unexpected. They made NFL roommate history, tore down an NFL color-barrier, and rebuilt a love-barrier that kept hate out.

When they first met, Piccolo spent most of his career living in the shadow of Sayers' athleticism. Piccolo wasn't as fast. He wasn't big enough. And Sayers had set a high athletic bar. Piccolo could have given up. But, instead of wallowing in self-pity, he chose hard work and teamwork. It was a turning point in his career and it opened the door to something new—a true multicultural friendship. When Piccolo was battling cancer later in his career, Sayers once said, "I love Brian Piccolo, and I'd like all of you to love him, too. Tonight, when you hit your knees, please ask God to love him."

The pursuit of love is a command God gives all of us. When it's paired with grace and mercy it is unstoppable. It will not, *will not*, <u>will not</u> in any way fail to complete its task nor let you down. So, strain for love and it will come. Work with mercy; and you'll find charity and kindness nearby. Show grace because it imparts blessings that can help in times of need, Heb 4:15,16.

I thank God for giving us the one spiritual gift we need most for a harmonious life together in difficult times—Love. It's the glue that binds us. Love in action is self-control, patience, kindness, hope, endurance, and unselfishness. Without them we are nothing; we are declared unfit for the race; and will never take hold of the prize, because we will fail.

Unfortunately, there will only be a few individuals willing to push through hurt, pain, and challenging obstacles. When others say, "I can't," love says, "I will and I can." Loving through tough times together is hard. Forgiveness is hard. Reconciliation is hard. But love conquers all.

Let us Pray:
God, you said in your word that, "All the special gifts and powers from God will someday come to an end, but love goes on forever." Will you teach us how to love? It is one of your greatest gifts that we desperately need. It has the power to strengthen marriages, restore friendships, and conquer any obstacle we face. Because you love us so much, you gave your son to die on the cross in our place so that we may live. Thank you. Amen.

A Time to Reflect

After reading this chapter, what is God saying to you?

Day 11

"If you abide in me, and my words abide in you, ask whatever you wish and it shall be done for you." John 15:7

Abide in Jesus

Devotional scripture: 1 Cor 3:16-17

Recently I read an article on the *Sage Publication* website. It was about couples committed to each other, but are living in separate houses. The article implied one reason that people do this is to protect personal independence and reduce cohabitation risks. Even though this unconventional way of partnering apart isn't new to unmarried couples, it certainly can be challenging for married couples. Sharing finances and raising children is challenging enough, let alone managing this between two different households. The article goes on to state that age is not always a factor. Old and young alike are testing living together separately.

I believe the Bible gives us a different path to follow. In fact, cohabitating with the Holy Spirit under the same roof, is what the Holy Spirit is doing in our lives today. He cohabits the believer's body through good times and bad, in sickness and in health. He longs to advise us. He gives us wisdom to manage our finances and raise our children, not apart, but together.

Jesus communicated a similar sentiment in John 15:4-7. He mentioned that if you abide in Him, you can be sure that whatever you ask will be listened to and acted upon. In Christ, abiding is about remaining, dwelling, and enduring together with a powerful being that can move mountains.

I can't imagine being satisfied with living together apart from God. Compare the fellowship style in Exodus 40:34-38 with the fellowship style in John 15:6-10 and 1 Corinthians 3:16-17. In the Exodus' together-but-apart style, God's presence was visible; however, Moses couldn't come near God's glory when it filled the Tabernacle. They shared a common purpose, but it was lacking spiritual intimacy. In 1 Cor 3:16-17, the relationship was upgraded to the better-together living within the same human body and equipped with gifts handed out by the Spirit. These gifts can impart wisdom, knowledge, faith, gifts of healings, and more, not by living apart from the Spirit, but by the Spirit living within you.

45

While I understand the importance that mankind places on maintaining independence and enjoying exclusive control, I would rather live a lifetime getting to know the person that saw my imperfections, stubbornness, and failures, yet still chose me.

John 15:7-8 paraphrased: When you're joined intimately together, the union is sure to be abundant.

Let us Pray:
Holy Spirit, thank you for the sweet fellowship that all believers can have with you. Never leave us alone. Thank you for abiding, guiding, and teaching us along life's pathway. When we don't know what to do, allow your mindset to resonate within us. Amen.

A Time to Reflect

After reading this chapter, what is God saying to you?

Day 12

We all become like mirrors who reflect the Lord Jesus.

The Beauty of Me is You

Devotional scripture: 2 Corinthians 3:17-18

A plastic surgery transformation is probably the most extensive makeover a person will ever undertake. A lift here, a tuck there, together with a foundation coverup every day is how some create a beautiful appearance. However, a makeover isn't possible without first identifying and correcting a few flaws or habits that inadvertently enhanced our aging process over the years.

We hear about beautiful people achieving success, and living beautiful lives. Every day, their appearance and lifestyle are on full display. But their inward flaws, fears, and self-doubts are safely hidden away, desperately in need of a life-changing makeover. And not a makeover that droops as they age. They need an inward change, something permanent. Something that connects to a daily refreshing, empowering, equipping, and stretching when needed. But, isn't this true for all of us? At times, we all fall victim to projecting a certain image while hiding our more embarrassing and undesirable traits.

Something within us is compelling us to change. And once we respond, beauty will take on a whole new definition.

Our unattractive behaviors and conditions will be gone, and something new will appear. Freedom! Free from an old belief of what makes a person attractive. Free to accept ourselves as God made us. Free to live boldly for Christ – within and without. Free to allow the Holy Spirit to reveal His features through us. Because when God resides in you with authority, an invisible power transforms a dull life to radiant. It turns a *Fashion Fair* perfect-looking person into someone that reflects God's glory. We all become like mirrors who reflect the Lord Jesus.

Beauty should not solely be defined by our outward attractiveness, intellect, color, or our hourglass shape. It should also shine through by how we respond to God's Spirit. And in the end, we will have no beauty apart from Him. We'll be beautiful inside and out.

Let us Pray:

God, everything you made is good. We know this so well. But sometimes we feel in bondage to the world's standards. Help us to break free of our view of who we are. Help us to see ourselves as you see us. We are breathtaking in your sight. Thank you for shaping us for your purpose. Give us the courage to use our inward beauty to attract those that are lost and need to see the beauty of who you are. Amen.

A Time to Reflect

After reading this chapter, what is God saying to you?

Day 13

When you hear God's voice, respond.

Now is the Time

Devotional scriptures: Hebrews 3:1-10, Exodus 3:14

When the South stubbornly persisted in slavery in the mid-1800s, a hero by the name of Harriet Tubman appeared on the scene. Even though she was born a slave, God used her to lead hundreds of enslaved people to freedom, as a conductor, in the Underground Railroad. At first glance you would think she was an unlikely candidate. She was five feet tall, uneducated, a slave, a field worker, and a black woman. But in spite of her outward description, God used her to transport slaves to freedom. History records she made 19 trips in the Underground Railroad, freed over 750 slaves, and never lost anyone along the journey.

Even though she deserves many accolades for her selfless acts of bravery as a conductor, it's her ability to hear God that I want to celebrate today. It is recorded that she suffered a severe head injury due to a beating by a local slave owner, which led her to have dreams and visions. Without warning she would slip into a trancelike sleep. It was during these periods that God spoke vividly to her. In a movie entitled *Harriet*, her character stated that during these trances, she focused all of her attention on God's visions. She didn't always know what to do, but she always responded by acting immediately upon what she saw.

Tell me, how could a slave that couldn't read or write have the ability to "trance-port" into the presence of God? I must admit, the answer is beyond my human understanding. But what I do know is this: God took someone that society deemed as worthless, and revealed her usefulness in His plans for freedom. The *I am, who I am*, used Harriet to end a life in bondage for 750 people and allowed them to begin a new life as freed men and women. It was an effortless task on God's part. But it would take someone with Harriet's faith, belief, and sense of urgency to pull off.

Hebrews 3:7-8 expresses a similar urgency for responding when hearing from God. Paul's letter emphasizes a strong priority to act

TODAY, because *now is the time*. To support his argument, Paul quickly gave a history lesson about the ones traveling with Moses from Egypt. Unlike Harriet, they rebelled against God, they did not act on His command, and they had to wander in the desert for 40 years. So a caution is given to the believers to BEWARE. Don't fall into that same hardhearted, do-it-my-way mentality. Listen to God's voice and respond.

God speaking to believers started long before Harriet. There were others in the Bible who said yes to God's specialized method of communicating to them. Joseph had a dream, and responded by organizing a farming project that saved thousands from starvation. God spoke to Gideon using a fleece, and Gideon led a trimmed-down army to victory. He spoke to Moses from a burning bush, and Moses freed his people from slavery. He spoke to His disciples through His son. And, now we can hear His voice every day in the Bible. Little by little we see God synchronizing His method of speaking to us *prior to* Jesus, *with* Jesus, and *after* Jesus with the ultimate goal of always being connected to us.

This ability to hear God doesn't require you be a prophet or a preacher or a disciple. You just need to be a believer and a listener. Occasionally, I hear people say, *I am not sure how to hear God's voice.* Believe, me, I truly understand. Even I sometimes question my listening skills. So, to broaden our awareness about how others hear from God, I thought it would be interesting to ask ordinary female believers how they hear God speaking. In the paragraph below, I have summarized their responses.

I hear from God through…

> *…reading the scripture*

> *…praying*

> *…pausing isolating to a peaceful place*

> *…walking through my situation in confidence*

> *…recognizing an inner feeling of his presence*

> *…singing*

> *…asking others to pray*

...seeking advice from mature Christians

...being patient and waiting on God

*...making sure my decisions don't contradict
God's character and scripture.*

From the list above, reading the Bible, praying, and pausing were the top three responses.

While I believe God's method of speaking is not bound by man, things, or even the list above, the warning in Hebrews is still the same. When God speaks to you, you must be obedient. He is seeking believers that will listen, believe, and respond, *Here I am, Lord. Send me.*

Let us Pray:
God, help us to be doers of your word. Allow us to start with simple tasks that fit into our everyday living environment. As we grow, increase our action list beyond our familiar borders in a way that strengthen our confidence and impact others richly. We want to be working in agreement with and alongside you. Amen.

A Time to Reflect

After reading this chapter, what is God saying to you?

Day 14

Who can keep Christ's love from you? Absolutely no one or nothing can.

Power Source

Devotional scripture: Ephesians 3:17-18

Christmas time during the early 60s was a very exciting time for me. I was around eight years old. My belief in Santa Claus was in full bloom, and the only gift I nagged my mom for every day was the Hasbro, Inc *Operation* game. It was a game of skill. A life-like picture of a man's body with a large red-light bulb nose was the board layout. Slots in the shape of organs and bones were strategically positioned over the man's body. Within these slots were plastic bones and organs. The player had to remove each piece using a tweezer without touching the edges. If you touched the edge, a loud buzzer would sound, ending your turn.

However, this particular year, my mom gave me heartbreaking news. Santa Claus wouldn't be able to grant my Christmas wish. My ears heard her. My mind understood her. But it didn't change my wish list. I was committed to having this one gift. So when people asked, "What do you want for Christmas?" I would simply say, "The *Operation* game," unwavering and unchanged. And sure enough, on Christmas day, the one and <u>only</u> gift I received was the *Operation* game. I was over-the-top excited. Tearing off the paper, I quickly put all the pieces in their proper slots. Finally, after assembling the game, it was ready. I picked up the tweezers and carefully tried to remove a bone. Realizing I had touched the edge and heard no sound, I became concerned. So, I deliberately touched the edges over and over again. Still no buzzing sound. My game was broken; what a disaster! I repeated this trial-and-error scene all day. I finally received the one thing I wanted and it didn't function as advertised. It was the most disappointing Christmas I had ever had.

Reflecting back, I now realize my mom didn't know it was a battery-operated device. Without batteries, my skills as a player meant nothing. No buzzer would ever sound to warn me that I had touched the edge. No red light would beam from the nose as an added visual alert that I had short-circuited the game. And without these two important stimuli, the game could not offer the climax of excitement. Without power, the game was no longer desirable. It meant nothing without the power source.

Unlike the battery-less *Operation* game that I received, God's believers come packing with a built-in power source called the Holy Spirit. He's the one that energizes our life, communicates what He hears, and warns us before we falter. He becomes the red light and buzzer that we seek for guidance. He's a 24-hour, 7-days-a-week living energy source. Above everything, He uses His power to show us how much Christ loves and desires us.

Ephesians 3:17-19 supports this concept. These verses share Paul's deep and passionate prayer for you. He wants you to be rooted in your understanding of Christ's love, through the strength of the Spirit's holy-voltage power. If you know God's love, then you will be filled with the fullness of God. So the question is this: *With this kind of power, who can keep Christ's love from you?* Absolutely no one or nothing can. Will death and life troubles separate any believer from God's love? Not a chance! Not even our fears and worries can succeed. Because the Spirit's power within you is the resting place for His love that cannot be matched or taken away by anything. And that's a Hallelujah, God-buzzer Christmas moment to be thankful for!

Let us Pray:
God, you are such a good Father. After your Son died on the cross for our sins, you gave us the best gift ever in the Holy Spirit. Thank you. You went all-in to show that you will never leave or forsake us. Holy Spirit, fill us abundantly with your powerful presence. Give us the courage to follow your lead as you direct our path. Amen.

A Time to Reflect

After reading this chapter, what is God saying to you?

Day 15

As children of God, we share God's path.

Connections That Lead Home

Devotional scripture: Romans 8:1-17

S tudies have shown that learning new things and exposing yourself to new experiences play an important role in creating new brain connections. As we generate new thoughts and learn new thing, our neurons, which most folks call brain cells, send signals to neighboring neurons, creating new network connections. These connections have the potential to enhance our memory and more. Even though creating new network connections is particularly essential when we are young, the benefit doesn't exclude adults.

Unfortunately, there are also ways to negatively impact these brain connections. Inactivity and negative experiences over an extended period of time have the potential to prune or break away existing connections if unused. I envision the inactivity as junctures connected to loss, negative thinking, repetitive routines, or a toxic environment. All of these experiences may be indicators that an individual's future will look just like their present, if unchanged. No growth beyond the here and now. However, the juncture connected to learning new things has the potential to unleash breakthroughs past the "same ol, same ol" lack of growth.

Take the 12 disciples for example. The apprenticeship program that they enrolled in to become followers of Jesus was the first of its kind. Everything about it caused them to encounter new experiences, concepts, and knowledge to create neuron growth. Each day of learning was filled with the expectation to learn more. They grew in knowledge and branched out their faith networks.

Although invisible to the human eye at the time, it would be the most monumental training they would ever dare to achieve. What they learned was revolutionary. They were being pruned from the old path of following the law apart from Jesus, and connected to the new path where they would have direct relationship with Christ and be indwelled by the Holy Spirit.

Before Christ, they were ordinary men carrying out traditional and habitual tasks. With Christ, they became extraordinary men with new network connections empowered by the Holy Spirit. And this transformation is now available to all of us, because Jesus supersized their connection by dying on the cross and rising again so that all men will be able to find their way home.

So, let me just say, the potential for a full life still exists. An aged adult over 70, a barren life, a struggling community, and especially a dying career can be attached to life-giving roots raring to sprout up a fresh start and new faith networks. Active faith networks bear witness to the glory of God. People will know by your responses that your faith networks are created for something that's eternal, never-ending, and unceasing. To say it another way, people will see that you are wired beyond yourself and this world. Romans 8:17, also reminds us that as children of God we share God's path. It's a path of good and sometimes suffering "with" Him, but if you stay the course, it leads from your earthly home to your heavenly home.

Let us Pray:
God, as we read the prayer below, fill us with excitement about being a part of the family of God.

"This resurrection life you received from God is not a timid, grave-tending life. It's adventurously expectant, greeting God with a childlike 'What's next, Papa?' God's Spirit touches our spirits and confirms who we really are. We know who he is, and we know who we are: Father and children. And we know we are going to get what's coming to us—an unbelievable inheritance! We go through exactly what Christ goes through. If we go through the hard times with him, then we're certainly going to go through the good times with him!" Amen.

The Message Bible Romans 8:15-17

A Time to Reflect

After reading this chapter, what is God saying to you?

Day 16

There is a God-time for everything.

God's Timing

Devotional scripture: Haggai 1:2-5

Timing is everything! It's a common phrase I have heard for a long time. People say things like, "I am waiting on God's timing to do this or that," but sometimes our timing is drenched in procrastination, doubt, and fear. Even God asked in Haggai 1:2-5, "Why is everyone saying it is *not the right time* for rebuilding my Temple? asks the Lord. His reply to them is this: Is it then the right time for you to live in luxurious homes, when the Temple lies in ruins? Look at the result:" — TLB.

Yes, let's pause and look at their results. They planted much, but harvested little. They worked hard, but earned barely enough to put food on the table. After paying the bills, there wasn't money left over to buy a decent pair of shoes for their children. Their needs for the "right now" consumed them. They had survival-eyes instead of God-eyes. Survival-eyes look at the immediate needs. God-eyes look at God's purpose and vision. Survival-eyes put self-first. God-eyes put His mission first. Since, their vision was near-sighted, their self-preservation was too, and the Temple laid in ruin.

Why was life so hard for them? Why did they work so hard, but gained so little? This is God's answer. Haggai 1:9-10, "…Because my Temple lies in ruins, and you don't care. Your only concern is your own fine homes. That is why I am holding back the rains from heaven and giving you such scant crops."

Their lack was their own fault. They were the roadblock to their own success. But when they repented, things changed in a mighty way. God was with them and gave them the desire to finish the temple. Haggai 1:12-13, "… and the few people remaining in the land obeyed Haggai's message from the Lord their God; they began to worship him in earnest. Then the Lord told them (again sending the message through Haggai, his messenger), I am with you; I will bless you."

Consider your current ways. Many of us have lived comfortably, storing away for a rainy day, while some of us live day-to-day. Several have accomplished the heights of their dreams or careers while so many are still left behind. Some have gained wisdom and confidence but failed to share their knowledge with those who need it. Ask yourself this: what do you really care about? Make a list and be honest. Place a check beside everything that concerns God and a question mark by everything that concerns you. Now, do your best to remove the roadblock (You) and receive His blessings.

Let us Pray:
God, forgive us for always putting our needs ahead of you. We don't always know what's best for ourselves. Thank you for wanting something better for mankind. Help us to wait on your timing and seek your face. I pray we learn how to make our desires fit within your perfect timing. Amen.

A Time to Reflect

After reading this chapter, what is God saying to you?

Day 17

Stale living isn't living.

Indifference

Devotional scripture: Revelations 3

How would you feel if someone came up to you and *called you out* in front of your friends and family? "Calling you out" is an Ebonics term that means "to hold someone accountable." At the time of the *calling out* it became my favorite language to express how the things I tried desperately to hide were now being exposed during a Bible study class. The Bible leader asked us to select a church from the book of Revelations that we felt best represented us in that particular moment. The list of churches and the general message to them is summarized below.

The Church of Ephesus, Rev 2:4 — "You don't love me or each other as you did at first!"

The Church of Smyrna, Rev 2:10 — "Don't be afraid of what you are about to suffer... But if you remain faithful even when facing death, I will give you the crown of life."

The Church of Pergamum, Rev 2:14,16 — "...You tolerate some among you whose teaching is like that of Balaam, ...Repent of your sin, ..."

The Church of Thyatira, Rev 2:20 — "...you are permitting that woman—that Jezebel who calls herself a prophet—to lead my servants astray."

The Church of Sardis, Rev 3:1 — "...I know all the things you do, and that you have a reputation for being alive—but you are dead."

The Church at Philadelphia, Rev 3:10 — "...you have obeyed my command to persevere, ..."

The Church of Laodicea, Rev 3:16 — "...you are like lukewarm water, neither hot nor cold..."

And with an honest examination, I selected Laodicea because lukewarm living felt like indifferent living to me. God knew the real me, not the pretense I wanted everyone to believe by my outer appearance or my works. He knew the sum of me. I wasn't indifferent in every area of my life, but indifferent to things that really mattered to Him.

Indifferent people can complete a task or go through life with lack of enthusiasm, satisfied with the mediocre. Stale! Flavorless! I understand this, because sometimes the most any of us can do while raising children, or dealing with hardships, or trying to get food on the table is just to get through the dailiness of the day. And not just one day, but seemingly unending struggles. This type of repetition without purpose can rob you of the importance of what you are doing. Work becomes just work. And if you have no particular interest or concern or purpose; habitual work can give birth to indifference.

Indifferent (neither hot nor cold) is what I believe God called the Church of Laodicea in Revelations 3. He saw right through them. The Church of Laodicea had a braggadocious "me, myself, and I" mentality. They boasted about everything in their life as if they did it on their own. God challenged them to take a stand to be either hot or cold; look to Him for their success and run after Him. He wanted the quality of their life and the state of their condition to be more usable for Him. Then He could enjoy the distinctive quality of their life. Inward spirit-led quality.

Indifferent is what He said about me during a bible study class 8 years ago. And it's what He is saying about someone today reading this devotional. You think you can go it alone without anyone's help, but you are wrong. This type of thinking will leave you poor of spirit, naked from the covering of faith, and downright pitiful. But God is rich! He can heal your spiritual sight and cover your shame.

Let us Pray:
God, thank you for wanting the best for your children. Teach us how to live hot in every area of our lives. When you see indifference and stale living in our life, reveal it to us so we can repent of it. Redirect our thoughts, actions, and the full sum of ourselves to a hot way of living. Amen.

A Time to Reflect

After reading this chapter, what is God saying to you?

Day 18

Daniel 9:23, "As soon as you began to pray, a word went out, which I have come to tell you, for you are highly esteemed."

Pray Like Daniel

Devotional scripture: Daniel 9-10

In 2017, I submitted a donation request to a company asking for financial support for a nonprofit. The Vice President (VP) liked the proposal and asked me to submit a formal request through the appropriate channels. He was warm and his conversations felt light with a strong get-to-know-you vibe.

Unlike some managers, he made me feel like an equal with something to offer; even though I was the one doing the asking. We talked several times and he always gave me positive feedback. But suddenly there was silence for a few months. I called and left messages without any response. Weeks later, I received a rejection letter in the mail— thanks, but no thanks. It came as a total surprise. The response in the letter and my conversations with the Vice President were like night and day. It wasn't like I hadn't received dozens of rejection letters before. In the nonprofit business you learn early to expect more rejections than acceptance. But this was different. Somehow, I felt within my soul that God had given me this donation. I kept saying things like, "God gave this to me. What happened?" I prayed daily about it. And one day, I decided to call. After all, I at least deserved to know why I wasn't selected for the donation.

God's "Yes" was loud in my heart and, rejection letter or not, God has the final say. I called a general corporate number, and unbeknownst to me, I was talking to the VP's former secretary. She listened with compassion, and after I was done telling her about the situation, she told me that one week after my last conversation with the VP he had died. That was why he never got back to me.

Maybe it was her soothing voice, but she told me not to worry and she would share my story with the appropriate people. She was true to her word. Two weeks later I received a check in the mail for the amount promised. I was right. God had said "Yes." It was delayed, but found its way to me in a timely fashion. God had placed before me an open door that no one could shut. Without faith, that $1,000 would still be in the company's account.

Now fast forward to three years later. God is still reminding me about the importance of prayer. Once again, I am seeking opportunities for the same nonprofit. Every effort appears to be closing, but my experience and historical records have shown that for every problem there are multiple solutions.

SCRIPTURE

Daniel 9:3-6

3So I turned to the Lord God and pleaded with him in prayer and petition, in fasting, and in sackcloth and ashes. 4 I prayed to the Lord my God and confessed: "Lord, the great and awesome God, who keeps his covenant of love with those who love him and keep his commandments, 5 we have sinned and done wrong. We have been wicked and have rebelled; we have turned away from your commands and laws. 6 We have not listened to your servants the prophets, who spoke in your name to our kings, our princes and our ancestors, and to all the people of the land.

Daniel 9:23

23 As soon as you began to pray, a word went out, which I have come to tell you, for you are highly esteemed

After reading Daniel 9-10, it became clear to me that if you want to move a mountain (Matt 17:20), prayer will require a deeper dive. Fasting and humility (Dan 10:2-3) becomes an important factor.

Take a look at Daniel's approach to prayer. In chapter 9, he put himself front and center of the people's sin against God. He used words such as, "we" and "us," rather than, "they" or "them."

Not once did Daniel exclude himself from the sins committed against God. Daniel said *we* all are guilty, and are covered with *shame* in your presence. He appealed to God's mercy. What an example. He basically said, *do not respond for our self-centered sakes. We are wicked, disobedient, and shameful, but respond to clear your name. Bring glory to your name.*

How many of us would take on all or the same punishment alongside the worst of the worst to help someone else—Even if you didn't desire it?

Daniel's prayer is sacrificial. And when you pray sacrificially you obtain *God's express answers.* Read Danial 9:23.

"As soon as you began to pray, a word went out, which I have come to tell you, for you are highly esteemed."

No wonder he got God's attention on the first day of prayer. But he also got someone else's attention—Satan. When the enemy sees you growing in faith through prayer, sometimes life gets a little tougher.

After Daniel prayed, a spiritual war in the heavenly realm was actively at work trying to block Daniel's answer, Dan 10: 13-14. *It took 21 days for Daniel to receive God's message with the help of God's top officer, Michael. This reminded me of my situation. A "yes" was given and an answer was delayed.*

Eph 6:12 validates that our battles are not against humans but against evil rulers, or satanic beings in high places. Some of us would have given up after the first few days of prayers. But not Daniel. He knew God would answer him if he stayed prayerful. And he was right. In Heaven he received an instant response. On earth there was a delayed message received from God. In Heaven there was a spiritual battle. On earth there was a prayer meeting going on. The success of a heavenly victory is a committed relationship and a committed prayer life.

Keep praying. Know that the answer is on the way. It may have gotten hung up in a good fight, but the battle is not yours, it's God's.

Let us Pray:

God, forgive us of our sins. We all have fallen short in life and need forgiveness from a Holy God. Give us spiritual backbone to acknowledge our faults and seek forgiveness. Teach us to fight on our knees. And regardless of what the situation looks like, help us to trust you at all times. Amen.

A Time to Reflect

After reading this chapter, what is God saying to you?

Day 19

Lord, teach me how to pray sincerely and honestly.

Prayer

Devotional scripture: Matthew 6:9-13

Call me a sap, but I couldn't hold back the tears after watching a movie called *I Believe*. The enduring love that persisted through good and hard times got the best of me. Without spoiling the movie, I will just say, it reflected a quality of devotion that we need more of.

It's not uncommon for us to see devotion in a loving relationship between a wife and husband, or employees with strong work ethics committed to assignments and vigorous work schedules. We understand these types of devoted scenarios. They can be unwavering and constant. At its best, devotion can give birth to loyalty. What's more, loyal people will go the distance for the people they love.

When I think about the word devotion and how it's unwavering, I am reminded that it's not just a one-time experience. This type of loyalty is cultivated with a steadfastness and stick-to-itness all day and every day.

The day I wrote this, I decided to put myself to the test of devotion. I wanted to see just how successfully I could commit to one day of continuous prayer. After all, 1 Thessalonians 5:17 tells us to, "Always keep on praying." So I started this challenge bright and early. It began great. The first hour was spent in prayer. Afterwards, I posted scriptures around my house to help me pray them back to God. By midday I was listening to Christian speakers. *Way to go*, I thought. *Things are going well*. But was it really?

Although I enjoyed every bit of it, something was missing, intimacy. I had planned intimacy right out of the day, robbing me of the closeness I sought from God. My planned day was organized, intentional, and each activity was checked off. It wasn't like a normal day which is typically filled with the unexpected like family errors, friendly sparring conversations with my husband, or volunteer activities.

Quite frankly, I wanted a do-over. I wanted my normal day back with a small, but powerful change. What if I allowed the spirit to lead my normal day? What if I spent the rest of the day structuring prayer and the Holy Spirit into the midst of my everyday living? Reading Matthew 6:7-13 helped me to understand this better. This scripture teaches us not to be like those trying to get something from God based on how we pray or the way we pray. Prayer techniques don't impress Him. What impresses Him are specific, honest, sincere, and simple prayers.

Prayers like…

Lord help me.
Psalms 30:10 "Hear me, Lord; oh, have pity and help me."

God, I thank you for a new day.
Lamentations 3:23 "Great is his faithfulness; his loving-kindness begins afresh each day."

Lord, thank you that I was able to overcome this obstacle. Thank you for getting me back on track again.
Isaiah 29:24 "Those who got off-track will get back on-track, and complainers and whiners will learn gratitude." — MSG

Bless this day.
Psalms 34:1 "I will bless the Lord at all times; His praise shall continually be in my mouth."

Devotion to prayer also includes Bible study or praying for others. But there's no need to create a special artistry for getting it done. He loves you just as you are. And He knows when we are not being our authentic selves

Be you and weave your prayers into your lifestyle continually.

Let us Pray:
God, I thank you for teaching us how to pray. Your Word tells us to pray along these lines: "Our Father in heaven, we honor your holy

name. We ask that your kingdom will come now. May your will be done here on earth, just as it is in heaven. Give us our food again today, as usual, and forgive us our sins, just as we have forgiven those who have sinned against us. Don't bring us into temptation, but deliver us from the Evil One." Amen. Matthew 6:9-13-TLB

A Time to Reflect

After reading this chapter, what is God saying to you?

Day 20

Show your faith through action.

Blessings

Devotional scripture: James 2:18-20

The food pantry is one of the most likely places you will experience your faith in action. It's filled with survival stories and strength. As a volunteer, I have prayed with pantry recipients and heard many stories of sickness, diseases, homelessness, divorce, loss of job, and more. Even though many people need financial support, it's not something that comes up often in conversation. Most people want to know that someone is praying for them and they find comfort in knowing that the pantry is there at their time of need. But on one occasion, a woman I met for the first time told me her story of being on the verge of losing her home in a few days. She had lost her job and wasn't able to pay the rent. She was at the end of her rope and needed help. She had requested government assistance, but the response would not be timely enough to prevent eviction from her home. I prayed and made suggestions, but there were no solutions found in my efforts. Finally, I told her that I would check around and asked her to come back the following week.

Her first and most important need was a place to stay. I must admit, I considered asking my husband if she could stay with us for a few weeks, but I considered the dangers. The conversation with myself went something like this, *"How can you invite a complete stranger into your home without a recommendation from a reliable source? Do you know if she is on drugs? Will she be a threat? Does she have any mental challenges? And, is she trustworthy?"*

These were all sound and reasonable thoughts. But the greatest inner argument centered around my husband. I knew in advance that he wouldn't like the idea, and quite frankly, it bothered me also. I imagined what he would say. *You are out of your mind! Have you gone mad? Have they brainwashed you at that church?*

Years ago, God taught me the importance of maintaining harmony in my home for a long-lasting relationship. Thirty-eight years of marriage wasn't lost in my learning experience. Marriage taught me about sharing, agreeing, compromising forgiving, and more. Through this valuable experience and God's wisdom, He reminded me that, in order for it to work, this decision had to be 100% supported by both of us. Next, I asked a church member who rented out a room if he could take her in, but he had no vacancy. I wasn't getting anywhere and had exhausted all of my ideas. It was a dead end, so I moved to the next need, money for bills and groceries.

The food pantry provides a limited amount of food needs, but it doesn't include personal hygiene or toiletries or other home needs. Could I help in this area? Should I ask others to give? At first, I wasn't sure what to do, but a few things helped — prayer, persistent asking, persistent seeking, and listening. In a few days, God reminded me of the small amount of money that I was saving to offset some of my family reunion expenses. It wasn't much, but it was available for use. With money in hand, I returned to the food pantry with $100. It was just a drop in the bucket, but I hoped it would help. I handed the money to her without revealing the amount, she thanked me, and left.

Side Bar: After the fact, I learned that the USDA reported the average cost of food per month for women between the ages of 19 to 50 is approximately $165 per month.

Many months had passed by, and I had long forgotten about the incident. Life was back to normal pantry duties, until one of the workers told me someone was insisting on seeing the African American lady that waited on her during her last visit. There were only 2 minority workers on duty that day, so I went. As I was approaching the car, I didn't recognize her at first. Her demeanor was positive, her face bright, and her tone uplifting. Immediately, she started telling me stories of her recovery to normalcy. Her story included highlights about receiving aid, finding an affordable apartment, having the apartment furnished with a table and bed (which was just enough), and finding a job. I was so happy for her. It was exciting to see how God was working behind the scenes for good even when I didn't see it or had forgotten about it.

God encouraged both of us that day. But the one thing that stood out the most in her testimony was what she said at the end. "When no one else believed me, you did." So now she plans to help someone else in the same way. Wow! Look at how God works. It wasn't about the money. Let's get real. The amount I gave her wouldn't sustain long-term needs. God was really looking for one person to believe Him. And today, He is still seeking that one person to hear Him and act. When we act in obedience, we open up opportunities for God's blessings to pass from person-to-person-to-person. And sometimes that one person will return to give Him glory.

Obedience » opens up the potential for God's blessings » that transforms a life » that benefits others » and leads to thankfulness.

Let us Pray:
God, thank you for the many blessings you have given us. Show us how to use your blessings to bless others. Provide opportunities for us to nurture our spiritual gifts so that we can walk fully into our purpose. Teach us a James 2:18-20 type of living. "But someone may well say, 'You have faith and I have works; show me your faith without the works, and I will show you my faith by my works.' You believe that [God is one. You do well; the demons also believe, and shudder. But are you willing to acknowledge, you foolish person, that faith without works is useless?" Amen.

A Time to Reflect

After reading this chapter, what is God saying to you?

Day 21

God's plans are to prosper you and not to harm you.

Dream's Eternal

Devotional scripture: Genesis 37:5-7

Are you familiar with the word *oneirology*? It's such a peculiar word. At first glance, you might think it means the study of oneself. But, it's actually the scientific study of dreams. The focus is primarily on the dream process. In 1951, a man name Aserinsky discovered the sleep stage when dreams actually occur. With the use of technology, his graph identified what is known as rapid eye movement (REM). Conducting a sleep experiment on his son, Aserinsky noticed a lot of activity with the equipment indicating that his son was alert and looking around. But when he checked, his son was asleep. It was an amazing scientific discovery. He was able to pinpoint during which stage dreams actually occurred, but not why we dream.

While the question of why we dream is more challenging and may never be fully understood, the Bible does give us insights into prophetic dreams. With all of the technological strides we have made, no graph can identify a prophetic dream. Especially like the one written about in Genesis 37:5-7. Scripture states, *"Joseph had a dream. When he told it to his brothers, they hated him even more. He said, 'Listen to this dream I had. We were all out in the field gathering bundles of wheat. All of a sudden my bundle stood straight up and your bundles circled around it and bowed down to mine.'* After hearing Joseph's dream, his brothers were furious, because the dream implied that Joseph would rule over them. At the time his brothers hated him for what is dreamed, but in the end, it certainly came true by the Dream Giver. God was preparing him for what was to come and how to save His people.

And what about today? Can God still speak to us in our dreams? It certainly isn't beyond His ability. Listen to this modern-day dream. *I was returning home with my husband. As our house came into view, we noticed all of our neighbors standing outside, sobbing. We were bewildered by the scene. But as we turned into our driveway, we immediately knew why. The front door to my home was wide open. It gave a straight view from the front door to the back door. And what I saw was heart breaking. Every bit of our furniture and belongings was gone. And the same thing had happened to everyone in our neighborhood. It was a scene straight out of the story* How the Grinch Stole Christmas! *Nothing in our house was left. Not a chair, not a table, not even a picture.* I am not saying that this was a prophetic dream. It was more likely due to thoughts about the Christmas season, but it did remind me of Matt 6:19-20. This scripture cautions us not to store up stuff that can decay or be stolen. Instead, store things with an eternal shelf-life. Love lasts forever and never fails. Leading others to Christ has eternal value. Shedding light on dark situations is life-giving.

We are all created to be dreamers. It's hardwired into our sleep process. But remember, not all dreams have Godly connections. Some are brought on by fears, daily activities, or what we eat. The Dream Giver REM stage will be Bible-centered and proven. It leads to reflection and causes us to pause. In my case, my dream caused me to think about what's really important. And it isn't the inanimate objects all around me or under my Christmas tree that are important. It is my family. It's being physical and spiritually healthy. And it's about getting to know God better. Tell me. What are you dreaming about these days?

Let us Pray:
God, thank you for the home you created for your children in Heaven. You have closed the deal and given us the keys to Heaven. The down payment has been made. No additional negotiations are needed. No fees are required. Jesus paid it all. So even when the grass withers or the sun refuses to shine, believers will be with God forever in Heaven. And that's something to dream about. Amen.

A Time to Reflect

After reading this chapter, what is God saying to you?

Day 22

Seek God's voice in everything you do.

Battle-Ready Words

Devotional scripture: Hebrews 4:12

When facing pitfalls in life, sometimes you need a collection of battle-ready words specific to the task at hand. Using battle-ready words has the potential to pull down strongholds that limit or restrict your success. Battle-ready words are a form of self-talk to change your thought process from negative to positive. They speak life and healing instead of death and doubt. They focus your attention from what's impossible to what's possible.

And if you want to know where to find free battle-ready words, check out 2 Timothy 3:16-17. Paul points us to a biblical resource full of empowerment. There's nothing like it. It reads, "All Scripture is inspired by God and beneficial for teaching, for rebuke, for correction, for training in righteousness; so that the man or woman of God may be fully capable, equipped for every good work."

Reciting God's word creates the right atmosphere. It sets an intimate ambiance of trust between you and God. It doesn't matter if the setting is passionate or unemotional. Sincerity of heart is what really matters.

Start by creating your own list of battle scriptures. It's a successful tactic for rolling back the old and inviting the new. It puts the enemy on notice that your faith is in God. On your own, you may fail, but with God nothing is impossible.

> With God's help we shall do mighty things, for he will trample down our foes.
> Psalms 60:12
>
> Don't fail me, Lord, for I am trusting you.
> Psalms 25:2
>
> Is anything too hard for God? Genesis 18:14

At the same time, it's okay to be encouraged by words of wisdom and phrases that uplift. That's why, after hearing the rally call of the first

WWII African American pilots in a movie called *Red Tails*, I couldn't resist adding it to my list of favorite phrases. I don't know for sure if the quote is true, but it echoed as battle-ready words to me. Prior to the airmen's fighting mission, they said, "To the last plane, to the last bullet, to the last minute, to the last man, we fight! We fight! We fight!"

These men traveled a long way for the privilege of serving as American pilots. It was not only a World War to be won against Nazi Germany, it was also a fight for greater equality in America. Black airmen were viewed inferior, flew inferior planes, and were given hand-me down equipment. However, none of it lessened their desire to serve.

I can't imagine how the wartime tensions affected their abilities to perform. They were trained to be the best. They could dazzle you with their ability to fly in unison. But still, they needed more to drown fear's whispers. Banding together, using phrases that uplift, was the final flying skill that made them battle-ready. "To the last plane, to the last bullet, to the last minute, to the last man, we fight! We fight! We fight!".

Although their words don't directly mention God, don't miss the presence of God in their trust. God's presence in any situation can carry your petitions straight to the throne of God. Maybe that's why, as reported in 2007, over their 15,000 missions as bomber, they maintained a near-perfect record.

So, by all means, practice self-talk that invokes God's involvement, but more importantly, use God's words. It is full of living power. "For the word of God is alive and active. Sharper than any double-edged sword, it penetrates even to dividing soul and spirit, joints and marrow; it judges the thoughts and attitudes of the heart. Hebrews 4:12."

Let us Pray:
God, help us to believe your word. It has the power to break physical and emotional bondage. Help us to cling to your word until it produces a harvest of deliverance, peace, and comfort. Amen.

A Time to Reflect

After reading this chapter, what is God saying to you?

Author

Brenette Wilder

Brenette Wilder is a member of Evangel Church, Kansas City, a mother of three daughters, and a wife. Brenette earned a Chemical Engineering degree from the University of Arkansas in Fayetteville and retired from Honeywell FM&T in 2017.

In 2005, she founded a nonprofit organization, *Kansas City Teen Summit (KCTS)*, to help disengaged youth become more involved in STEM education (science, technology, engineering, math). A percentage of the proceeds from each book purchase will be used to support *Kansas City Teen Summit's* summer program.

She first wrote *Dream Number 4*, a non-fiction book. It's about her call to fulfill her fourth dream on a list created during a women's retreat—writing for God.

Brenette still resides in the Kansas City, Missouri area with her husband. She spends most of her time volunteering, reading, and writing her personal thoughts after spending time in the Bible.

Contact Brenette Wilder at nettedtogether@gmail.com to schedule a book review. You can learn more about KCTS at www.kansascityteensummit.org.

CPSIA information can be obtained
at www.ICGtesting.com
Printed in the USA
LVHW080751191122
733589LV00031B/1631

9 781737 811206